General Information

Many of the products used in this pattern book can be purchased from local craft, fabric and variety stores, or from the Annie's Attic Needlecraft Catalog (see Customer Service information on page 20).

Rooster

SKILL LEVEL

INTERMEDIATE

FINISHED SIZES

Towel Topper: 7 inches square, excluding button lp

Dishcloth: 7 inches square

MATERIALS

- Peaches & Crème medium (worsted) weight cotton yarn (2½ oz/122 yds/ 71g per ball):
  1 ball each #10 yellow and #89 camel
- Size H/8/5mm crochet hook
- Sewing needle
- Matching sewing thread
- ¾-inch yellow button: 1
- Kitchen dish towel

GAUGE

16 sc = 4 inches; 16 sc rows = 4 inches

PATTERN NOTE

Join with slip stitch as indicated unless otherwise stated.

SPECIAL STITCH

Cross-stitch (cross-st): Sk next st, sc in next st, sc in st just sk.

INSTRUCTIONS

TOWEL TOPPER

Row 1 (RS): With camel, ch 25, sc in 2nd ch from hook and in each ch across, **do not turn.** Fasten off. *(24 sc)*

Row 2 (RS): Join yellow with sc in first st, **cross-st** *(see Special Stitch)* across, ending with sc in last st, turn. Fasten off.

Row 3: Join camel with sc in first st, sc in each st across, turn. Fasten off.

Row 4: Join yellow with sc in first st, cross-st across, ending with sc in last st, turn.

Rows 5–22: [Rep rows 3 and 4 alternately] 9 times.

Row 23: Join camel with sc in first st, sc in each st across, turn. Fasten off.

BORDER

Rnd 1: Now working in rnds, with RS facing, join yellow with sc in first st, sc in each st across, ch 2 *(corner)*, working in ends of rows, sc in each row across, ch 2 *(corner)*, working in starting ch on opposite side of row 1, sc in each ch across, ch 2 *(corner)*, working in ends of rows, sc in each row across, ch 2 *(corner)*, **join** *(see Pattern Note)* in beg sc.

Rnd 2: Ch 1, [sc in each st across to corner ch sp, 3 sc in corner ch sp] 3 times, sc in each st across to corner ch sp, (2 sc, ch 10, sl st in last st, sc) in last corner ch sp *(button lp)*, join in beg sc. Fasten off.

FINISHING

Fold hand towel in half. Run double stand of sewing thread through towel at fold.

Fold Towel Topper from corner to corner to form triangle with hanging lp at top.

Sew button to opposite corner. Button to secure.

Gather towel to fit fold of Towel Topper and sew in place.

DISHCLOTH

Row 1 (RS): With camel, ch 25, sc in 2nd ch from hook and in each ch across, **do not turn.** Fasten off. *(24 sc)*

Row 2 (RS): Join yellow with sc in first st, **cross-st** *(see Special Stitch)* across, ending with sc in last st, turn. Fasten off.

Row 3: Join camel with sc in first st, sc in each st across, turn. Fasten off.

Row 4: Join yellow with sc in first st, cross-st across ending with sc in last st, turn.

Rows 5–22: [Rep rows 3 and 4 alternately] 9 times.

Row 23: Join camel with sc in first st, sc in each st across, turn. Fasten off.

BORDER

Rnd 1: Now working in rnds, with RS facing, join yellow with sc in first st, sc in each st across, ch 2 *(corner)*, working in ends of rows, sc in each row across, ch 2 *(corner)*, working in starting ch on opposite side of row 1, sc in each ch across, ch 2 *(corner)*, working in ends of rows, sc in each row across, ch 2 *(corner)*, **join** *(see Pattern Note)* in beg sc.

Rnd 2: Ch 1, sc in each st around with 3 sc in each corner ch sp, join in beg sc. Fasten off. ∎

Spring Garden

SKILL LEVEL

INTERMEDIATE

FINISHED SIZES

Towel Topper: 3 x 10¼ inches
Dishcloth: 7½ x 8 inches

MATERIALS

- Crème De La Crème medium (worsted) weight cotton yarn (2½ oz/ 126 yds/71g per ball):
  1 ball each #0870 cornflower blue, #0910 wood violet, #0200 sunshine, #0887 royal blue and #0625 brite green
- Size H/8/5mm crochet hook or size needed to obtain gauge
- Sewing needle
- Matching sewing thread
- ¾-inch blue button: 1
- Kitchen dish towel

GAUGE

15 sc = 4 inches; 15 sc rows = 4 inches

PATTERN NOTES

Chain-1 at beginning of row or round does not count as first half double crochet unless otherwise stated.

Join with slip stitch as indicated unless otherwise stated.

SPECIAL STITCH

Cross-stitch (cross-st): Sk next st, sc in next st, sc in last sk st.

INSTRUCTIONS

TOWEL TOPPER

RING

Row 1 (RS): With cornflower blue, ch 4, hdc in 2nd ch from hook and in each ch across, turn. *(3 hdc)*

Rows 2–28: Ch 1 *(see Pattern Notes)*, hdc in first st and in each st across, turn. At end of last row, fasten off.

BORDER

Rnd 1: Now working in rnds, with RS facing, join cornflower blue in top right-hand corner, ch 1, sc in each st across, ch 2 *(corner)*, sc in end of each row across, ch 2 *(corner)*, working in starting ch on opposite side of row 1, sc in each ch across, ch 2 *(corner)*, sc in end of each row across, ch 2 *(corner)*, **join** *(see Pattern Notes)* in beg sc. Fasten off.

Rnd 2: Join violet with sc in corner ch-2 sp before 1 short end, ch 2, sc in same ch sp, *sc in each st across to corner ch sp, (sc, ch 2, sc) in corner ch-2 sp, working down length, cross-st across to next corner ch sp**, (sc, ch 2, sc) in corner ch sp, rep from * around, ending last rep at **, join in beg sc.

Row 3: Holding Ring RS tog, working through both thicknesses sl st short ends tog. Fasten off.

Turn RS out and fold in half.

Insert towel in Ring.

HANGING STRIP

Row 1: With cornflower blue, ch 7, hdc in 2nd ch from hook and in each ch across, turn. *(6 hdc)*

Rows 2–34: Ch 1, hdc in first st and in each st across, turn. At end of last row, fasten off.

BORDER

Rnd 1: Now working in rnds, with RS facing, join cornflower blue in top right-hand corner, ch 1, sc in each st across, ch 2 *(corner)*, sc in end of each row across, ch 2 *(corner)*, working in starting ch on opposite side of row 1, sc in each ch across, ch 2 *(corner)*, sc in end of each row across, ch 2 *(corner)*, **join** (see *Pattern Notes*) in beg sc. Fasten off.

Rnd 2: Join violet with sc in corner ch-2 sp before 1 short end, ch 2, sc in same ch sp, *sc in each st across to corner ch sp, (sc, ch 2, sc) in corner ch-2 sp, working down length, cross-st across to next corner ch sp**, (sc, ch 2, sc) in corner ch sp, rep from * around ending last rep at **, join in beg sc. Fasten off.

HANGING LOOP

Join violet with sc in 4th st on 1 short end of Hanging Strip, ch 8, sc in next st. Fasten off.

SIDE BORDER

Working across 1 long edge, with RS facing, join sunshine with sc in corner ch-2 sp, sc in each st across, sc in corner ch sp. Fasten off.

Rep on opposite side.

FINISHING

Sew button on RS of Hanging Strip at bottom center opposite end from Hanging Loop.

Insert Hanging Strip through Ring and close with button.

FLOWER

Rnd 1: With sunshine, ch 4, sl st in first ch to form ring, ch 1, [sc in ring, ch 2] 8 times, join in beg sc. Fasten off.

Rnd 2: Join royal blue with sc in any ch-2 sp, (3 dc, sl st) in same ch sp, (sc, 3 dc, sl st) in each ch sp around, join in beg sc. Fasten off.

LEAF
MAKE 2.

With green, ch 4, (dc, 2 tr, ch 3, sl st in last tr, 2 tr, 2 dc) in 4th ch from hook. Fasten off.

Sew 1 Leaf to each side of Flower.

Sew Flower and Leaves to Hanging Strip as shown in photo.

DISHCLOTH

Row 1: With cornflower blue, ch 27, hdc in 2nd ch from hook and in each ch across, turn. *(26 hdc)*

Rows 2 & 3: Ch 1, hdc in first st and in each st across, turn. At end of last row, fasten off.

Row 4: Join sunshine in first st, ch 1, hdc in first st and in each st across, turn. Fasten off.

Row 5: Join violet with sc in first st, **cross-st** (see *Special Stitch*) across ending with sc in last st, turn. Fasten off.

Row 6: Join sunshine in first st, ch 1, hdc in first st and in each st across, turn. Fasten off.

Row 7: Join cornflower blue in first st, ch 1, hdc in first st and in each st across, turn.

Rows 8–10: Ch 1, hdc in first st and in each st across, turn. At end of last row, fasten off.

Row 11: Join sunshine in first st, ch 1, hdc in first st and in each st across, turn. Fasten off.

Row 12: Join violet with sc in first st, cross-st across ending with sc in last st, turn. Fasten off.

Row 13: Join sunshine in first st, ch 1, hdc in first st and in each st across, turn. Fasten off.

Row 14: Join cornflower blue in first st, ch 1, hdc in first st and in each st across, turn.

Rows 15–17: Ch 1, hdc in first st and in each st across, turn. At end of last row, fasten off.

Row 18: Join sunshine in first st, ch 1, hdc in first st and in each st across, turn. Fasten off.

continued on page 16

Chef

SKILL LEVEL

INTERMEDIATE

FINISHED SIZES

Towel Topper: 2⅝ x 11¼ inches, excluding button lp

Dishcloth: 7¼ inches square

MATERIALS

- Crème De La Crème medium (worsted) weight cotton yarn (2½ oz/ 126 yds/71g per ball):
  1 ball #0001 white
- Aunt Lydia's Fashion Crochet size 3 crochet cotton (150 yds per ball):
  1 ball #6 scarlett
- Size H/8/5mm crochet hook or size needed to obtain gauge
- Sewing needle
- Matching sewing thread
- ¾-inch white button: 1
- Kitchen dish towel

GAUGE

(Sc, ch 2, sc) 8 times = 5 inches; 8 pattern rows = 5 inches

PATTERN NOTE

Join with slip stitch as indicated unless otherwise stated.

INSTRUCTIONS
TOWEL TOPPER
RING

Row 1 (RS): With scarlett, ch 41, (sc, ch 2, sc) in 2nd ch from hook, [sk next 2 chs, (sc, ch 2, sc) in next ch] across, turn.

Rows 2–4: Sl st in first ch-2 sp, ch 1, (sc, ch 2, sc) in same ch sp and in each ch sp across, turn. At end of last row, fasten off.

Row 5: Working in starting ch on opposite side of row 1, join scarlett with sc in first ch, ch 2, sc in same ch, [sk next 2 chs, (sc, ch 2, sc) in next ch] across, turn.

Rows 6–8: Sl st in first ch-2 sp, ch 1, (sc, ch 2, sc) in same ch sp and in each ch sp across, turn.

Row 9: Fold ends RS tog, working through both thicknesses, sl st ends of rows tog forming ring. Fasten off. Turn RS out and fold in half.

Insert towel in Ring.

HANGING STRAP

Rnd 1: With white, ch 41, (sc, ch 2, sc) in 2nd ch from hook, [sk next 2 chs, (sc, ch 2, sc) across, ch 2, working on opposite side of ch, (sc, ch 2, sc) in first ch, [sk next 2 chs, (sc, ch 2, sc) in next ch] across, ch 2, join (see Pattern Notes) in beg sc.

Rnd 2: Sl st in first ch-2 sp, ch 1, *(sc, ch 2, sc) in each of next 14 ch-2 sps, ch 2, (sc, ch 2, sc) in ch sp at end, ch 2, rep from * around, join in beg sc.

Rnd 3: Sl st in first ch-2 sp, ch 1, (sc, ch 2, sc) in each of next 15 ch-2 sps, ch 2, (sc, ch 2, sc) in next ch-2 sp, ch 2, (sc, ch 2, sc) in each of next 16 ch-2 sps, [ch 2, (sc, ch 2, sc) in next ch-2 sp] twice, join in beg sc. Fasten off.

continued on page 16

Sunflower

SKILL LEVEL

INTERMEDIATE

FINISHED SIZES

Towel Topper:
Ring = 5 inches in diameter
Hanging Strap: 5¼ inches, excluding Ring
and button lp
Dishcloth: 8 inches square

MATERIALS

- Crème De La Crème medium
  (worsted) weight cotton yarn (2½ oz/
  126 yds/71g per ball):
    1 ball each #0001 white, #0620 green
    shadow, #0625 brite green and
    #0200 sunshine
- Size H/8/5mm crochet hook or size
  needed to obtain gauge
- Sewing needle
- Matching sewing thread
- ¾-inch white button: 1
- Kitchen dish towel
- 4-inch metal ring
- Stitch markers

GAUGE

14 sc = 4 inches; 13 rows = 4 inches

PATTERN NOTES

Join with slip stitch as indicated unless
otherwise stated.

Chain-3 at beginning of rows or rounds
counts as first double crochet unless
otherwise stated.

INSTRUCTIONS
TOWEL TOPPER
RING

Rnd 1: With white, ch 4, 12 dc in 4th
ch from hook, *(first 3 chs count as first

dc)*, **join** *(see Pattern Notes)* in 3rd ch of beg
ch-3. *(13 dc)*

Rnd 2: Ch 3 *(see Pattern Notes)*, dc in same st,
2 dc in each st around, join in 3rd ch of beg
ch-3. *(26 dc)*

Rnd 3: Ch 1, 2 sc in first st, [sc in each of next
2 sts, 2 sc in next st] around, sc in last st, join
in beg sc. *(35 sc)*

Rnd 4: Holding 4-inch ring in back of work, sc around 4-inch ring (*see Fig. 1*), ch 1, 2 sc in each of first 18 sts (*mark center 8 sts*), leaving rem ring unworked and working in sts only, sc in each of rem 17 sts, join in beg sc. Fasten off. (*53 sc*)

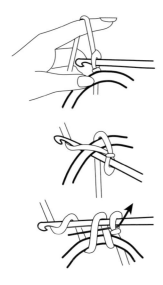

**Single Crochet Around Ring
Fig. 1**

Rnd 5: Join sunshine with sc in **front lp** (*see Stitch Guide*) of first st, sc in front lp of each st around, join in beg sc. Fasten off.

Rnd 6: Working in front lps, join green shadow with sc in front lp of first st, ch 3, sl st in top of last st, [sc in each of next 2 sts, ch 3, sl st in top of last st] around, join in beg sc. Fasten off.

HANGING STRAP
Row 1: With RS facing, working in **back lps** (*see Stitch Guide*) of each of 8 marked sts on rnd 4, join white with sc in first st, sc in each of next 7 marked sts, remove marker, leaving rem sts unworked, turn. (*8 sc*)

Rows 2–20: Ch 1, sc in each st across, turn.

Row 21: Ch 1, **sc dec** (*see Stitch Guide*) in first 2 sts, sc in each st across, sc dec in last 2 sts, turn. (*6 sc*)

Row 22: Ch 1, sc dec in first 2 sts, sc in each of next 2 sts, sc dec in last 2 sts, turn. (*4 sc*)

Row 23: Ch 1, sc dec in first 2 sts, sc dec in last 2 sts, turn. (*2 sc*)

Row 24: Ch 10 (*button lp*), sl st in last st. Fasten off.

SUNFLOWER
Rnd 1: With brite green, ch 4, 9 dc in 4th ch from hook (*first 3 chs count as first dc*), join in 3rd ch of beg ch-4. Fasten off. (*10 dc*)

Rnd 2: Join sunshine in first st, ch 1, (hdc, dc, tr, ch 2, sl st in top of last tr, sl st down side of last tr) in same st, [ch 1, (hdc, dc, tr, ch 2, sl st in top of last tr, sl st down side of last tr) in next st] around, join in joining sl st. Fasten off.

FINISHING
Sew Sunflower to center of Ring as shown in photo.

Fold Hanging Strap to back and sew button to row 2.

Button to secure.

Place towel through portion of unworked ring.

DISHCLOTH
Row 1 (RS): With green shadow, ch 26, sc in 2nd ch from hook and in each ch across, turn. Fasten off. (*25 sc*)

Row 2: Join sunshine with sc in first st, sc in each st across, turn. Fasten off.

Row 3: Join brite green with sc in first st, sc in next st, ch 4, sl st in top of last st, [sc in each of next 2 sts, ch 4, sl st in top of last st] across, ending with sc in last st, turn. Fasten off.

Row 4: Join green shadow in first st, ch 3, [sc in next ch-4 sp, sk next st, dc in next st] across, turn. Fasten off.

Row 5: Join sunshine with sc in first st, sc in each st across, turn. Fasten off.

Rows 6–20: [Rep rows 3–5 consecutively] 5 times.

continued on page 17

Teddy Bear

SKILL LEVEL

INTERMEDIATE

FINISHED SIZES

Towel Topper: Hanging Strap is 3¾ x 8⅝ inches, excluding button lp

Dishcloth: 8 inches square

MATERIALS

- Crème De La Crème medium (worsted) weight cotton yarn (2½ oz/126 yds/71g per ball): 1 ball #0625 brite green
- Size H/8/5mm crochet hook
- Size H/8/5mm afghan crochet hook or size needed to obtain gauge
- Sewing needle
- Matching sewing thread
- ¾-inch flower button: 1
- Kitchen dish towel

GAUGE

Size H Afghan hook: 18 afghan sts = 4 inches; 17 afghan rows = 4 inches

Size H crochet hook: 3 sc rows = 1¼ inches

PATTERN NOTE

Join with slip stitch as indicated unless otherwise stated.

SPECIAL STITCHES

Work lps off hook: Yo, pull through 1 lp on hook (see A), [yo, pull through 2 lps on hook] across leaving 1 lp on hook at end of row (see B).

Afghan stitch (afghan st): Sk first vertical bar, pull up lp in next vertical bar (see C), pull up lp in each vertical bar across to last vertical bar, for last st, insert hook in last bar and st directly behind it (see D) at same time, yo, pull lp through, work lps off hook.

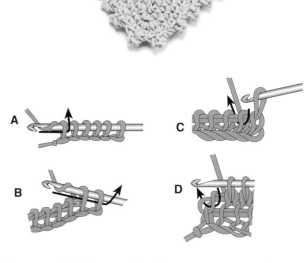

Decrease (dec): Insert hook in next 2 vertical bars, yo, pull lp through.

INSTRUCTIONS
TOWEL TOPPER
RING

Row 1: With size H afghan hook, ch 9, leaving all lps on hook, pull up lp in each ch across, **work lps off hook** (see Special Stitches).

Row 2: [With yarn in front, **afghan st** (see Special Stitches), with yarn in back, afghan st] across, work lps off hook.

Row 3: [With yarn in back, afghan st, with yarn in front, afghan st] across, work lps off.

Rows 4–31: [Rep rows 2 and 3 alternately] 14 times. At end of last row, fasten off.

Fold strip with RS tog, working through both thicknesses, sl st first and last rows tog.

Turn RS out and fold in half to form circle. Insert towel in Ring.

HANGING STRAP

Row 1: With afghan hook, ch 13, leaving all lps on hook, pull up lp in each ch across, work lps off hook.

Row 2: [With yarn in front, afghan st, with yarn in back, afghan st] across, work lps off hook.

Row 3: [With yarn in back, afghan st, with yarn in front, afghan st] across, work lps off hook.

Rows 4–25: [Rep rows 2 and 3 alternately] 11 times.

Row 26: [With yarn in front, afghan st, with yarn in back, afghan st] across, work lps off hook.

Row 27: With yarn in front, **dec** (see Special Stitches), [with yarn in back, afghan st, with yarn in front, afghan st] 4 times, with yarn in back, dec (11 lps), work lps off hook.

Row 28: With yarn in front, dec, [with yarn in back, afghan st, with yarn in front, afghan st] 3 times, with yarn in back, dec (9 lps), work lps off hook.

Row 29: With yarn in front, dec, [with yarn in back, afghan st, with yarn in front, afghan st] twice, with yarn in back, dec (7 lps), work lps off hook.

Row 30: With yarn in front, dec, with yarn in back, dec, with yarn in front, dec (4 lps), work lps off hook.

Row 31: Sl st in each vertical bar across. **Do not fasten off.**

BORDER

Working around outer edge in ends of rows, with size H crochet hook, ch 1, sc in end of each of next 2 rows, ch 3, sl st in top of last sc, [sc in end of each of next 2 rows, ch 3, sl st in top of last sc] across, working in starting ch on opposite side of row 1, [sc in each of next 2 chs, ch 3, sl st in top of last sc] 6 times, [sc in end of each of next 2 rows, ch 3, sl st in top of last sc] across, sc in each of first 2 sts, ch 10 (button lp), sc in each of last 2 sts, **join** (see Pattern Note) in beg sc. Fasten off.

Sew button to center bottom of Hanging Strap.

With WS facing insert Hanging Strap through center of Ring. Button to secure.

DISHCLOTH

Row 1: With size H afghan hook, ch 25, leaving all lps on hook, pull up lp in each ch across, **work lps off hook** (see Special Stitches).

Row 2: [With yarn in front, **afghan st** (see Special Stitches), with yarn in back, afghan st] across, work lps off hook.

Row 3: With yarn in back, afghan st, with yarn in front afghan st] across, work lps off hook.

Rows 4–21: [Rep rows 2 and 3 alternately] 9 times.

Row 22: [With yarn in front, afghan st, with yarn in back, afghan st] across, work lps off hook.

Row 23: [With yarn in back, sl st in next vertical bar, with yarn in front, sl st in next vertical bar] across. **Do not fasten off.**

continued on page 17

Pastel Rose

SKILL LEVEL

INTERMEDIATE

FINISHED SIZES

Towel Topper: 7¼ inches square
Dishcloth: 8 inches square

MATERIALS

- Crème De La Crème medium (worsted) weight cotton yarn (solid: 2½ oz/126 yds/71g multi: 2oz/ 99 yds/57g per ball):
    1 ball each #0625 brite green, #0910 wood violet, #0936 lemontones and #0001 white
- Size H/8/5mm crochet hook
- Sewing needle
- Matching sewing thread
- ¾-inch purple button: 1
- Kitchen dish towel

GAUGE

Towel Topper: 16 sc = 4 inches; 20 sc rows = 4 inches

Dishcloth: 15 sc and chs = 4 inches; 16 pattern rows = 4 inches

PATTERN NOTE

Join with slip stitch as indicated unless otherwise stated.

INSTRUCTIONS

TOWEL TOPPER

Row 1: With green, ch 23, sc in 2nd ch from hook and in each ch across, turn. *(22 sc)*

Rows 2–29: Ch 1, sc in each st across, turn. At end of last row. Fasten off.

BORDER

Rnd 1: With RS facing, join white with sc in first st, sc in each st across, ch 2 *(corner)*, working in ends of rows, [sc in each of next 3 rows, sk next row] 7 times, sc in last row, ch 2 *(corner)*, working in starting ch on opposite side of row 1, sc in each ch across, ch 2 *(corner)*, working in ends of rows, [sc in each of next 3 rows, sk next row] 7 times, sc in last row, ch 2 *(corner)*, **join** *(see Pattern Note)* in beg sc. Fasten off.

Rnd 2: Join violet with sc in any corner ch sp, sc in same ch sp, ch 3, sl st in last st, [sc in each of next 2 sts, ch 3, sl st in last st] around with (2 sc, ch 3, sl st in last st) in each corner ch sp around to last corner ch sp, (sc, ch 10—*button lp*, sl st in last st, sc) in last corner ch sp, join in beg sc. Fasten off.

PASTEL ROSE

Rnd 1: With lemontones, ch 4, sl st in first ch to form ring, ch 1, [sc in ring, ch 3] 8 times, join in beg sc. Fasten off.

Rnd 2: Join violet with sc in any ch sp, (hdc, dc, hdc, sc) in same ch sp, (sc, hdc, dc, hdc, sc) in each ch sp around, join in beg sc. Fasten off.

continued on page 17

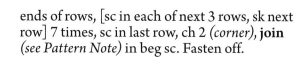

Basic
Navy & White

SKILL LEVEL

INTERMEDIATE

FINISHED SIZES
Towel Topper: 4½ x 8½ inches
Dishcloth: 8 inches square

MATERIALS
- Crème De La Crème medium (worsted) weight cotton yarn (2½ oz/ 126 yds/71g per ball):
  2 balls #0856 navy
  1 ball #0001 white
- Size H/8/5mm crochet hook
- Sewing needle
- Matching sewing thread
- ¾-inch navy button: 1
- Kitchen dish towel

GAUGE
15 sc = 4 inches; 19 sc rows = 4 inches

PATTERN NOTE
Join with slip stitch as indicated unless otherwise stated.

INSTRUCTIONS
TOWEL TOPPER
Row 1: With navy, ch 19, sc in 2nd ch from hook and in each ch across, turn. (*18 sc*)

Rows 2–24: Ch 1, sc in each st across, turn. At end of last row, fasten off.

BORDER
Rnd 1: Now working in rnds and in ends of rows, join white with sc in first st, sc in each st across, ch 2 (*corner*), [sc in end of each of next 4 rows, sk next row] 4 times, sc in end of each of next 4 rows, ch 2 (*corner*), working in starting ch on opposite side of row 1, sc in each ch across, ch 2 (*corner*), [sc in end of each of next 4 rows, sk

next row] 4 times, sc in end of each of next 4 rows, ch 2 (*corner*), **join** (*see Pattern Note*) in beg sc. Fasten off.

Rnd 2: Join navy with sc in last corner ch sp, ch 2, sc in same ch sp, sc in each st around with (sc, ch 2, sc) in each corner ch sp, join in beg sc. Fasten off.

Rnd 3: Join white with sc in first corner ch sp, ch 10 (*button lp*), sc in same ch sp, sc in each st

continued on page 18

Daisy

SKILL LEVEL

INTERMEDIATE

FINISHED SIZES
Towel Topper:
Ring = 4½ inches in diameter
Hanging Strap = 2⅛ x 5 inches, excluding
    button lp
Dishcloth: 8¼ inches square

MATERIALS
- Crème De La Crème medium (worsted) **4 MEDIUM**
  weight cotton yarn (solids: 2½ oz/
  126 yds/71g; multis: 2oz/99 yds/57g
  per ball):
    1 ball each #0943 French country ombre,
    #0870 cornflower blue, #0887 royal blue,
    #0625 brite green, #0200 sunshine and
    #0001 white
- Size H/8/5mm crochet hook
- Sewing needle
- Matching sewing thread
- ¾-inch blue button: 1
- Kitchen dish towel
- 4-inch metal ring
- Stitch markers

GAUGE
Towel Topper: 15 sc = 4 inches; 19 sc rows = 4
    inches

Dishcloth: 15 pattern rows = 4 inches

PATTERN NOTES
Join with slip stitch as indicated unless
    otherwise stated.

Chain-3 at beginning of row or round counts as
    first double crochet unless otherwise stated.

INSTRUCTIONS
TOWEL TOPPER
RING
Rnd 1: With royal blue, ch 4, 12 dc in 4th ch
from hook (*first 3 chs count as first dc*), **join** (*see
Pattern Notes*) in 3rd ch of beg ch-3. (*13 dc*)

Rnd 2: Ch 3 (*see
Pattern Notes*), dc
in same st, 2 dc in
each st around, join
in 3rd ch of beg
ch-3. (*26 dc*)

Rnd 3: Ch 1, 2 sc in
first st, [sc in each
of next 2 sts, 2 sc in
next st] around, sc
in last st, join in beg
sc. (*35 sc*)

Rnd 4: Holding ring
in back of work, sc
around ring and in
sts at same time (*see
Fig. 1*), ch 1, 2 sc in

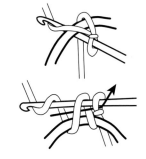

**Single Crochet Around Ring
Fig. 1**

each of first 17 sts, mark center 8 sts, leaving rem ring unworked, working in sts only, sc in each of last 18 sts, join in beg sc. Fasten off. *(52 sc)*

Rnd 5: Working in **front lps** *(see Stitch Guide)*, join cornflower blue with sc in first st, sc in next st, ch 2, sl st in last st, [sc in each of next 2 sts, ch 2, sl st in last st] around, join in beg sc. Fasten off.

HANGING STRAP
Row 1: Working in rem lps of marked 8 sts on rnd 4, with RS facing, join cornflower blue with sc in first marked st, sc in each of next marked 7 sts, turn. Remove markers. *(8 sc)*

Rows 2–20: Ch 1, sc in each st across, turn.

Row 21: Ch 1, **sc dec** *(see Stitch Guide)* in first 2 sts, sc in each of next 4 sts, sc dec in last 2 sts, turn. *(6 sc)*

Row 22: Ch 1, sc dec in first 2 sts, sc in each of next 2 sts, sc dec in last 2 sts, turn. *(4 sc)*

Row 23: Ch 1, sc dec in first 2 sts, sc dec in last 2 sts, turn. *(2 sc)*

Row 24: Sl st in first st, ch 10 *(button lp)*, sl st in last st. Fasten off.

Sew button in center of WS on row 1 on Hanging Strap.

DAISY
Rnd 1: With sunshine, ch 2, 8 sc in 2nd ch from hook, join in beg sc. Fasten off.

Rnd 2: Working in front lps, join white in first st, (ch 8, sl st) twice in same st, (sl st, {ch 8, sl st} twice) in each st around, join in beg sl st. Fasten off.

LEAVES
Rnd 3: Working in **back lps** *(see Stitch Guide)* of rnd 1, join green with sc in any st, ch 7, sc in next st, [sc in next st, ch 7, sc in next st] around, join in beg sc. *(4 ch sps)*

Rnd 4: Sl st in first ch sp, ch 1, (sc, hdc, dc, tr, ch 3, sl st in last st, tr, dc, hdc, sc) in same ch sp and in each ch sp around, join in beg sc. Fasten off.

Sew Daisy to center front of Ring.

Insert towel through unworked part of metal ring.

DISHCLOTH
Row 1: With French country ombre, ch 26, sc in 2nd ch from hook, [dc in next ch, sc in next ch] across, turn. *(25 sts)*

Row 2: **Ch 3** *(see Pattern Notes)*, [sc in next st, dc in next st] across, turn.

Row 3: Ch 1, sc in first st, [dc in next st, sc in next st] across, turn.

Rows 4–25: [Rep rows 2 and 3 alternately for pattern] 11 times. At end of last row, fasten off.

BORDER
Rnd 1: With RS facing, join French country ombre with sc in first st, sc in each st across, ch 2 *(corner)*, working in ends of rows, sc in end of each row across, ch 2 *(corner)*, working in starting ch on opposite side of row 1, sc in each ch across, ch 2 *(corner)*, working in ends of rows, sc in end of each row across, ch 2 *(corner)*, join in beg sc. Fasten off.

Rnd 2: Join royal blue with sc in any corner ch sp, ch 2, sc in same ch sp, *[ch 1, sk next st, sc in next st] across to next corner, sk next st**, (sc, ch 2, sc) in corner ch sp, rep from * around, ending last rep at **, join in beg sc. Fasten off.

Rnd 3: Join cornflower blue with sc in any corner ch sp, ch 2, sc in same ch sp, *sc in next st, [sc in next ch sp, ch 2, sl st in last st, sc in next st] across to next corner**, (sc, ch 2, sc) in next corner ch sp, rep from * around, ending last rep at **, join in beg sc. Fasten off. ■

Espresso

SKILL LEVEL

INTERMEDIATE

FINISHED SIZES

Towel Topper:
Ring = 4 inches in diameter
Hanging Strap = 2¼ x 5¼ inches, excluding
  button lp
Dishcloth: 7½ x 8 inches

MATERIALS

- Peaches & Crème medium (worsted) weight cotton yarn (2½ oz/122 yds/ 71g per ball):
    1 ball each #1 white and #89 camel
- Size H/8/5mm crochet hook or size needed to obtain gauge
- Sewing needle
- Matching sewing thread
- ¾-inch white button: 1
- Kitchen dish towel
- 4-inch metal ring
- Stitch markers

MEDIUM

GAUGE

6 V-sts = 4 inches; 10 V-st rows = 4 inches

PATTERN NOTE

Join with slip stitch as indicated unless otherwise
  stated.

SPECIAL STITCHES

Beginning popcorn (beg pc): Ch 3 *(counts as first dc)*, 4 dc in same place, drop lp from hook, insert hook in 3rd ch of beg ch-3, pull dropped lp through, ch 1 to close.

Popcorn (pc): 5 dc in place indicated, drop lp from hook, insert hook in first dc of group, pull dropped lp through, ch 1 to close.

V-stitch (V-st): (Sc, ch 3, sc) in place indicated.

INSTRUCTIONS
TOWEL TOPPER
RING

Rnd 1: With white, ch 4, sl st in first ch to form ring, **beg pc** *(see Special Stitches)* in ring, ch 3, [**pc** *(see Special Stitches)* in ring, ch 3] 5 times, **join** *(see Pattern Note)* in beg pc. Fasten off. *(6 pc)*

Rnd 2: Join camel in first pc, ch 1, 3 hdc in same st, *dc in sp between pc in ring**, 3 hdc in next st, rep from * around, ending last rep at **, join in beg hdc. Fasten off. *(24 inches)*

Rnd 3: Join white with sc in first st, ch 2, sc in same st, sk next st, [**V-st** *(see Special Stitches)* in next st, sk next st] around, join in beg sc.

Rnd 4: Holding metal ring in back of work, sc around ring *(see Fig. 1)* as you work in sts, ch 1, sc in first st, [2 sc in next ch sp, sc in each of next 2 sts] 6 times, 2 sc in next ch sp, sc in next st, *(mark center 8 sts)* leaving rem ring unworked and working in sts only, [sc in next st, 2 sc in next ch sp, sc in next st] around, join in beg sc. **Do not fasten off.**

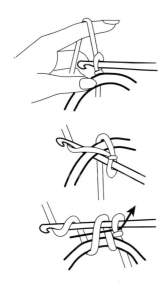

**Single Crochet Around Ring
Fig. 1**

Rnd 5: Working in **front lps** *(see Stitch Guide)*, ch 1, sc in first st **changing colors** *(see Stitch Guide)* to camel, [sc in next st changing to white, sc in next st changing to camel] around changing to white in last st, join in beg sc. Fasten off.

HANGING STRAP
Row 1: Working in back lps of rnd 4, join camel with sc in first marked st, sc in each of next 7 marked sts, remove markers, turn. *(8 sc)*

Rows 2–20: Ch 1, sc in each st across, turn.

Row 21: Ch 1, **sc dec** *(see Stitch Guide)* in first 2 sts, sc in each st across ending with sc dec in last 2 sts, turn. *(6 sc)*

Row 22: Ch 1, sc dec in first 2 sts, sc in each of next 2 sts, sc dec in last 2 sts, turn. *(4 sc)*

Row 23: Ch 1, sc dec in first 2 sts, sc dec in last 2 sts, turn. *(2 sc)*

Row 24: Ch 10 *(button lp)*, sl st in last st. Fasten off.

Sew button in center of row 1 on WS of Hanging Strap. Place button lp around button.

Place towel in unworked part of metal ring.

DISHCLOTH
Row 1: With camel, ch 29, **V-st** *(see Special Stitches)* in 2nd ch from hook, [sk next 2 chs, V-st in next ch] across, turn. Fasten off. *(10 V-sts)*

Row 2: Join white with sc in first ch sp, ch 2, sc in same ch sp, V-st in ch sp of each V-st across, turn. Fasten off.

Row 3: Join camel with sc in first ch sp, ch 23, sc in same ch sp, V-st in ch sp of each V-st across, turn. Fasten off.

Rows 4–15: [Rep rows 2 and 3 alternately] 6 times. At end of last row, fasten off.

BORDER
Rnd 1: Now working in rnds, with RS facing, join white with sc in first ch sp, ch 2, sc in same ch sp, V-st in ch sp of each V-st across to last V-st, (V-st, ch 3, sc) in ch sp of last V-st, working in ends of rows, sk first row, V-st in next row, [sk next row, V-st in next row] 6 times, sk last row, (V-st, ch 3, sc) in first ch, [sk next ch, V-st in next ch] across to last ch, (V-st, ch 3, sc) in last ch, working in ends of rows, sk first row, V-st in next row, [sk next row, V-st in next row] 6 times, sk last row, (sc, ch 3) in same st as first sc, join in beg sc.

Rnd 2: Sl st in first ch sp, ch 1, V-st in same ch sp and in ch sp of each V-st and in each ch-3 sp around, join in beg sc. Fasten off. ■

Spring Garden
continued from page 4

Row 19: Join violet with sc in first st, cross-st across ending with sc in last st, turn. Fasten off.

Row 20: Join sunshine in first st, ch 1, hdc in first st and in each st across, turn. Fasten off.

Row 21: Join cornflower blue in first st, ch 1, hdc in first st and in each st across, turn.

Rows 22 & 23: Ch 1, hdc in first st and in each st across, turn. At end of last row, fasten off.

Rnd 24: Working around outer edge, ch 1, hdc in first st and in each st across to corner, ch 2 *(corner)*, hdc in end of each row across to corner, ch 2 *(corner)*, working in starting ch on opposite side of row 1, hdc in each ch across to corner, ch 2 *(corner)*, hdc in end of each row across to corner, ch 2 *(corner)*, join in beg hdc.

Rnd 25: Ch 1, hdc in first st, hdc in each st around with 3 hdc in each corner ch sp, join in beg hdc. Fasten off.

FLOWER
Rnd 1: With sunshine, ch 4, sl st in first ch to form ring, ch 1, [sc in ring, ch 2] 8 times, join in beg sc. Fasten off.

Rnd 2: Join royal blue with sc in any ch-2 sp, (3 dc, sl st) in same ch sp, (sc, 3 dc, sl st) in each ch sp around, join in beg sc. Fasten off.

LEAF
MAKE 2.
With green, ch 4, (dc, 2 tr, ch 3, sl st in last tr, 2 tr, 2 dc) in 4th ch from hook. Fasten off.

Sew 1 Leaf to each side of Flower.

Sew Flower and Leaves to center of Dishcloth as shown in photo. ■

Chef
continued from page 5

Rnd 4: Join scarlett with sc in beg ch-2 sp, ch 2, sc in same ch sp, (sc, ch 2, sc) in each of next 15 ch-2 sps, (sc, ch 7, sc) in next ch-2 sp *(ch-7 is button lp)*, (sc, ch 2, sc) in each of next 21 ch-2 sps, join in beg sc. Fasten off.

Sew button to end of Hanging Strap opposite button lp.

Insert 1 end of Hanging Strap through Ring, button to secure.

DISHCLOTH
Row 1: With white, ch 29, (sc, ch 2, sc) in 2nd ch from hook, [sk next 2 chs, (sc, ch 2, sc) in next ch] across, turn.

Rows 2–18: Sl st in first ch-2 sp, ch 1, (sc, ch 2, sc) in same ch sp and in each ch-2 sp across, turn.

BORDER
Rnd 1: Now working in rnds, sl st in first ch-2 sp, ch 1, (sc, ch 2, sc) in same ch sp and in each ch-2 sp across, ch 2, working in ends of rows, (sc, ch 2, sc) in end of first row, [sk next row, (sc, ch 2, sc) in end of next row] 7 times, sk next 2 rows, (sc, ch 2, sc) in end of last row, ch 2, working in starting ch on opposite side of row 1, (sc, ch 2, sc) in first ch, [sk next 2 chs, (sc, ch 2, sc) in next ch] across, ch 2, working in ends of rows, (sc, ch 2, sc) in end of first row, [sk next row, (sc, ch 2, sc) in end of next row] 7 times, sk next 2 rows, (sc, ch 2, sc) in end of last row, ch 2, join in beg sc. Fasten off.

Rnd 2: Join scarlett with sc in first ch sp, ch 2, sc in same ch sp, (sc, ch 2, sc) in each ch sp around, join in beg sc. Fasten off. ■

Sunflower

continued from page 7

Row 21: Join brite green with sc in first st, sc in next st, ch 4, sl st in top of last st, [sc in each of next 2 sts, ch 4, sl st in top of last st] across, ending with sc in last st, turn. Fasten off.

Row 22: Join green shadow in first st, ch 3, [sc in next ch-4 sp, sk next st, dc in next st] across, turn. Fasten off.

BORDER
Rnd 1: Now working in rnds, with RS facing, join sunshine in first st, ch 1, hdc in same st and in each st across, ch 2 (corner), working in ends of rows, 2 hdc in first row, [sk next sc row, hdc in next sc row, 2 hdc in next dc row] 6 times, sk next sc row, hdc in next sc row, 2 hdc in last sc row, ch 2 (corner), working in starting ch on opposite side of row 1, hdc in each ch across, ch 2 (corner), working in ends of row, 2 hdc in end of first row, [sk next sc row, hdc in next sc row, 2 hdc in next dc row] 7 times, ch 2 (corner), join in beg hdc.

Rnd 2: Ch 1, hdc in each st around with 6 hdc in each corner ch sp, join in top of beg hdc. Fasten off. ■

Teddy Bear

continued from page 9

BORDER
Rnd 1: Now working in rnds and in ends of rows, with size H crochet hook, ch 1, sc in each st across, ch 2 (corner), sc in end of each row across, ch 2 (corner), working in starting ch on opposite side of row 1, sc in each ch across, ch 2 (corner), sc in end of each row across, ch 2 (corner), **join** (see Pattern Note) in beg sc.

Rnd 2: Ch 1, sc in each st around with 3 sc in each corner ch sp, join in beg sc.

Rnd 3: Ch 1, sc in each of first 2 sts, ch 3, sl st in top of last sc, [sc in each of next 2 sts, ch 2, sl st in top of last sc] around, join in beg sc. Fasten off. ■

Pastel Rose

continued from page 10

Rnd 3: Working behind rnd 2, join lemontones with **bpsc** (see Stitch Guide) around any sc on rnd 1, ch 4, [bpsc around next st on rnd 1, ch 4] around, join in beg bpsc. Fasten off.

Rnd 4: Join white with sc in any ch-4 sp, (hdc, 3 dc, hdc, sc) in same ch sp, (sc, hdc, 3 dc, hdc, sc) in each ch sp around, join in beg sc. Fasten off.

FINISHING
Fold hand towel in half. Run double stand of sewing thread through towel at fold.

Fold Towel Topper from corner to corner to form triangle with button lp at top.

Sew button to opposite corner. Button to secure.

Sew Pastel Rose to side with button lp for front.

Gather towel to fit fold of Towel Topper and sew in place.

DISHCLOTH

Row 1: With white, ch 26, sc in 2nd ch from hook and in each ch across, turn. Fasten off. *(25 sc)*

Row 2: Join violet with sc in first st, [ch 1, sk next st, sc in next st] across, turn. Fasten off.

Row 3: Join white with sc in first st, sc in each ch sp and in each st across, turn. Fasten off.

Row 4: Join green with sc in first st, [ch 1, sk next st, sc in next st] across, turn. Fasten off.

Row 5: Join white with sc in first st, sc in each ch sp and in each st across, turn. Fasten off.

Row 6: Join violet with sc in first st, [ch 1, sk next st, sc in next st] across, turn. Fasten off.

Rows 7–26: [Rep rows 3–6 consecutively] 5 times.

Row 27: Join white with sc in first st, sc in each ch sp and in each st across, turn. Fasten off.

BORDER

Rnd 1: With RS facing, join green in first st, hdc in same st and in each st across, ch 2 *(corner)*, working in ends of rows, [hdc in each of next 3 rows, sk next row] 6 times, hdc in each of last 3 rows, ch 2 *(corner)*, working in starting ch on opposite side of row 1, hdc in each ch across, ch 2 *(corner)*, working in ends of rows, [hdc in each of next 3 rows, sk next row] 6 times, hdc in each of last 3 rows, ch 2 *(corner)*, **join** *(see Pattern Note)* in beg hdc. Fasten off.

Rnd 2: Working in each st and in each ch, join violet with sc in first st, sc in next st, ch 3, sl st in last st, [sc in each of next 2 sts or chs, ch 3, sl st in last st] around, join in beg sc. Fasten off. ■

Basic Navy & White
continued from page 11

around with 2 sc in each corner ch sp, join in beg sc. Fasten off.

FINISHING
Fold hand towel in half. Run double stand of sewing thread through towel at fold.

Fold Towel Topper from corner to corner to form triangle with hanger at top.

Sew button to opposite corner. Button to secure.

Gather towel to fit fold of Towel Topper and sew in place.

DISHCLOTH

Row 1: With navy, ch 25, sc in 2nd ch from hook and in each ch across, turn. *(14 sc)*

Rows 2–32: Ch 1, sc in each st across, turn. At end of last row, fasten off.

BORDER

Rnd 1: Now working in rnds and in ends of rows, join white with sc in first st, sc in each st across, ch 2 *(corner)*, [sc in end of each of next 4 rows, sk next row] 6 times, sc in end of each of next 2 rows, ch 2 *(corner)*, working in starting ch on opposite side of row 1, sc in each ch across, ch 2 *(corner)*, [sc in end of each of next 4 rows, sk next row] 6 times, sc in end of each of next 2 rows, ch 2 *(corner)*, **join** *(see Pattern Note)* in beg sc. Fasten off.

Rnd 2: Join navy with sc in last corner ch sp, ch 2, sc in same ch sp, sc in each st around with (sc, ch 2, sc) in each corner ch sp, join in beg sc. Fasten off.

Rnd 3: Join white with sc in first corner ch sp, sc in same ch sp, sc in each st around with 2 sc in each corner ch sp, join in beg sc. Fasten off. ■

Stitch Guide
For more complete information, visit **FreePatterns.com**

ABBREVIATIONS

beg	begin/beginning
bpdc	back post double crochet
bpsc	back post single crochet
bptr	back post treble crochet
CC	contrasting color
ch	chain stitch
ch-	refers to chain or space previously made (i.e., ch-1 space)
ch sp	chain space
cl	cluster
cm	centimeter(s)
dc	double crochet
dec	decrease/decreases/decreasing
dtr	double treble crochet
fpdc	front post double crochet
fpsc	front post single crochet
fptr	front post treble crochet
g	gram(s)
hdc	half double crochet
inc	increase/increases/increasing
lng	long
lp(s)	loop(s)
MC	main color
mm	millimeter(s)
oz	ounce(s)
pc	popcorn
rem	remain/remaining
rep	repeat(s)
rnd(s)	round(s)
RS	right side
sc	single crochet
sk	skip(ped)
sl st	slip stitch
sp(s)	space(s)
st(s)	stitch(es)
tog	together
tr	treble crochet
trtr	triple treble crochet
WS	wrong side
yd(s)	yard(s)
yo	yarn over

Chain—ch: Yo, pull through lp on hook.

Slip stitch—sl st: Insert hook in st, pull through both lps on hook.

Single crochet—sc: Insert hook in st, yo, pull through st, yo, pull through both lps on hook.

Front post stitch—fp: Back post stitch—bp: When working post st, insert hook from right to left around post st on previous row.

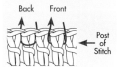

Back   Front

← Post of Stitch

Front loop—front lp Back loop— back lp

Front Loop   Back Loop

Half double crochet— hdc: Yo, insert hook in st, yo, pull through st, yo, pull through all 3 lps on hook.

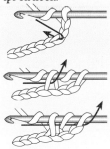

Double crochet—dc: Yo, insert hook in st, yo, pull through st, [yo, pull through 2 lps] twice.

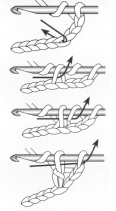

Change colors: Drop first color; with 2nd color, pull through last 2 lps of st.

Treble crochet—tr: Yo twice, insert hook in st, yo, pull through st, [yo, pull through 2 lps] 3 times.

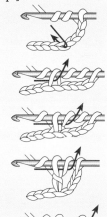

Double treble crochet—dtr: Yo 3 times, insert hook in st, yo, pull through st, [yo, pull through 2 lps] 4 times.

Single crochet decrease (sc dec): (Insert hook, yo, draw lp through) in each of the sts indicated, yo, draw through all lps on hook.

Example of 2-sc dec

Half double crochet decrease (hdc dec): (Yo, insert hook, yo, draw lp through) in each of the sts indicated, yo, draw through all lps on hook.

Example of 2-hdc dec

Double crochet decrease (dc dec): (Yo, insert hook, yo, draw loop through, draw through 2 lps on hook) in each of the sts indicated, yo, draw through all lps on hook.

Example of 2-dc dec

Example of 2-tr dec

Treble crochet decrease (tr dec): Holding back last lp of each st, tr in each of the sts indicated, yo, pull through all lps on hook.

US		UK
sl st (slip stitch)	=	sc (single crochet)
sc (single crochet)	=	dc (double crochet)
hdc (half double crochet)	=	htr (half treble crochet)
dc (double crochet)	=	tr (treble crochet)
tr (treble crochet)	=	dtr (double treble crochet)
dtr (double treble crochet)	=	ttr (triple treble crochet)
skip	=	miss

TOLL-FREE ORDER LINE or to request a free catalog (800) LV-ANNIE (800) 582-6643
Customer Service (800) AT-ANNIE (800) 282-6643, **Fax** (800) 882-6643
Visit anniesattic.com

We have made every effort to ensure the accuracy and completeness of these instructions.
We cannot, however, be responsible for human error, typographical mistakes or variations in individual work.

ISBN: 978-1-59635-212-4

1 2 3 4 5 6 7 8 9